Assessing and Improving Student Organizations

Student Workbook

Assessing and Improving Student Organizations

Student Workbook

Tricia Nolfi and Brent D. Ruben

STERLING • VIRGINIA

Published in association with ACPA and

**Advancing Campus Activities
in Higher Education**

Published by Stylus Publishing, LLC
22883 Quicksilver Drive
Sterling, Virginia 20166-2102

13-digit ISBN: 978-1-57922-414-1 (paper)

Printed in the United States of America

All first editions printed on acid free paper
that meets the American National Standards Institute
Z39-48 Standard.

Bulk Purchases

Quantity discounts are
available for use in workshops
and for staff development.
Call 1-800-232-0223

First Edition, 2010

10 9 8 7 6 5 4 3 2 1

AISO Student Workbook

This Workbook is intended to be used by participants during the AISO assessment and planning sessions. It is helpful to use it in tandem with Assessing and Improving Student Organizations: A Guide for Students. If you have questions during the process or need additional clarification, be sure to ask your Facilitator as he or she will have additional resources that may be helpful.

In using the Workbook you will note some icons on the pages.

✓ This symbol references where you can find more related information on the topic in the Student Guide

☺ This symbol indicates an idea or thought that you had

The Workbook is for your purposes, so be sure to write down notes, ideas, and thoughts as they come to you during the AISO process.

Congratulations on your commitment to improving your student organization and contributing to the enhancement of student life on your campus!

AISO Themes

☐ **Leadership.** Define, communicate, and model the vision and values to which the organization aspires, including a focus on the needs of members and external constituency groups.

☐ **Strategic Planning.** Translate aspirations into plans with clear, aggressive goals; see plans through to completion.

☐ **Constituent Focus.** Listen to and understand the needs and perspectives of the groups you serve. Develop an organization-wide service ethic; identify and close gaps.

☐ **Programs, Services, and Activities.** Identify, analyze, standardize, and continuously improve the quality and effectiveness of programs, activities, services, and processes to ensure that the highest possible standards are met.

✓ **Check it out:** Look in the *AISO Guide for Students* at pages xv–xvii for more information on this topic.

☺ **Idea:** _____

_____

_____

_____

_____

_____

_____

_____

_____

_____

_____

_____

_____

_____

AISO Themes

☐ **Membership and Organizational Climate.** Create a culture that encourages excellence, engagement, personal and career development, commitment, and pride. Reward and recognize performance and synchronize individual and organizational goals.

☐ **Assessment and Communication.** Assess the quality and effectiveness of your purpose-critical programs, activities and services, and of all other areas of organizational functioning. Effectively share information, knowledge, and expertise throughout the organization and beyond.

☐ **Outcomes and Achievements.** Gather evidence to track your progress and achievements, and use the information to guide decision making and improvements. Compare your achievements and accomplishments to those of peers and leaders. Tell your story.

✔ **Check it out:** Look in the *AISO Guide for Students* at pages xvi–xviii for more information on this topic.

☺ **Idea:** _____

Key Categories for Assessing and Improving Student Organizations

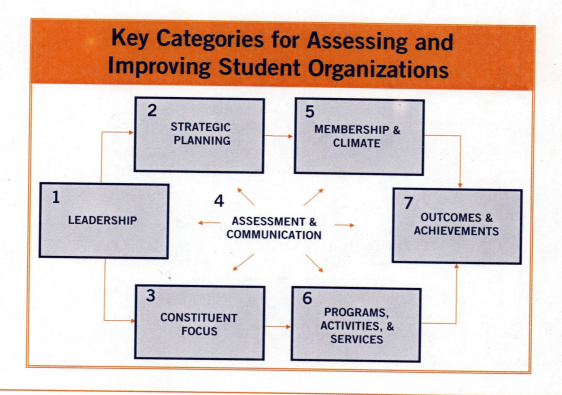

✓ **Check it out:** Look in the *AISO Guide for Students* at pages xvi–xviii for more information on this topic.

☺ **Idea:** _____

_____

_____

_____

_____

_____

_____

_____

_____

_____

_____

_____

_____

_____

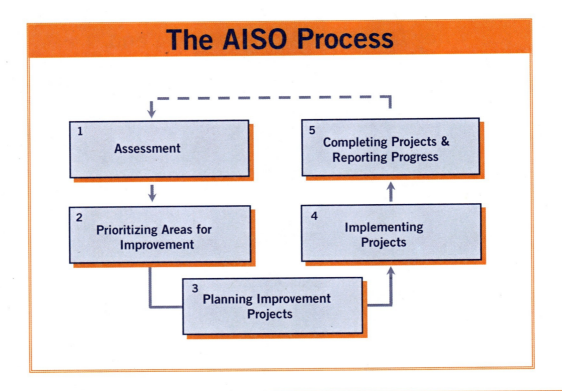

The AISO Process

1 Assessment	**5** Completing Projects & Reporting Progress
2 Prioritizing Areas for Improvement	**4** Implementing Projects
	3 Planning Improvement Projects

✓ **Check it out:** Look in the *AISO Guide for Students* at page xvi for more information on this topic.

☺ **Idea:** _____

Student Organization Profile
Topics to Be Considered

Description and Structure

List and Describe:
- Organization being assessed
- Purpose/mission
- Organizational and leadership structure
- Membership profile
- Organizational culture
- Advisory bodies
- Recent assessments, reviews, or planning activities
- Peers and leading organizations

Organizational Relationships

List and Describe:
- Groups and organizations benefiting from your programs, activities, and services
- Groups/organizations that are important to your program or organization
- Collaborators

Challenges and Opportunities

List and Describe:
- Comparison to similar campus programs or organizations
- Challenges
- Opportunities

✔ **Check it out:** Look in the *AISO Guide for Students* at pages xv–xviii for more information on this topic.

☺ **Idea:** _____

Who provides "the leadership" for your organization?

- ☐ The elected leader and his or her leadership team?
- ☐ The executive council?
- ☐ The governing council?
- ☐ The program chair or head?
- ☐ The general membership?

✓ **Check it out:** Look in the *AISO Guide for Students* at pages 5–10 for more information on this topic.

☺ **Idea:** _____

_____
_____
_____
_____
_____
_____
_____
_____
_____
_____
_____
_____

Percentage Rating Guide

Rating	Approach/Implementation	Outcomes and Achievements
100% to 90%	■ A superior approach; systematic and fully responsive to the category/item. ■ Fully implemented without significant weaknesses or gaps in any area. ■ Widely recognized leader in the category/item. ■ Systematic approach and commitment to excellence and continuous improvement fully ingrained in the student organization and its culture.	■ Exceptional documented, current, and sustained outcomes and achievements related to the mission, vision, values, plans and goals, as well as for programs, activities and services, and constituencies, membership and climate and all other categories. ■ Clear and documented evidence that the student organization is a leader in higher education.
80% to 70%	■ A well-developed, systematic, tested and refined approach in most areas, responsive to the overall purpose of the category/item. ■ A fact-based assessment and improvement process throughout most of the student organization with few significant gaps. ■ Innovative; recognized as a leader in the category/item. ■ Clear evidence of excellence and continuous improvement throughout most of the student organization and its culture.	■ Very good to excellent documented, current and sustained outcomes and achievements in most areas related to the mission, vision, values, plans and goals, as well as for programs, activities and services, and constituencies, membership and climate and all other categories. ■ Many to most current outcomes and trends evaluated against—and comparing favorably with—peer and leading student organizations.

☺ **Idea:** _____

_____

_____

_____

_____

_____

_____

_____

_____

_____

_____

_____

_____

Percentage Rating Guide

Rating	Approach/Implementation	Outcomes and Achievements
60% to 50%	■ An effective, systematic approach, responsive to the overall purpose of the category/item. ■ An approach that is well implemented in many areas, although unevenness and inconsistency may exist in some committees, task forces, etc. ■ A fact-based, systematic process in place for evaluating and improving effectiveness and efficiency in many areas. ■ Clear evidence of excellence and continuous improvement in many areas of the student organization and its culture.	■ Good to very good current and sustained outcomes and achievements documented in many areas. ■ Many current and sustained outcomes and achievements evaluated against—and comparing favorably with—peer and leading student organizations. ■ No pattern of poor outcomes or adverse trends in key areas.
40% to 30%	■ An effective, systematic approach, responsive to the basic purpose of the category/item. ■ An approach that is implemented in some areas, but with some committees, task forces, etc. in the early stages of implementation. ■ The beginning of a systematic approach to assessing and improving effectiveness and efficiency in some areas. ■ Clear evidence of excellence and continuous improvement in some areas of the student organization and its culture.	■ Current and sustained positive outcomes and achievements documented in some areas. ■ Early stages of developing trends and obtaining comparative information in some areas.

☺ **Idea:** _____

_____

_____

_____

_____

_____

_____

_____

_____

_____

_____

_____

_____

Percentage Rating Guide

Rating	Approach/Implementation	Outcomes and Achievements
20% to 10%	■ The beginnings of a systematic approach to basic purposes of the category/item. ■ Category criteria addressed in a few programs, services, activities and processes. may exist in some committees, task forces, etc. ■ Major implementation gaps that inhibit progress in achieving the basic purpose of category/item. ■ Clear evidence of excellence and continuous improvement in a few areas of the student organization and its culture.	■ Outcomes and achievements documented in a few areas. ■ Evidence of positive results and improvements in a few areas. ■ Minimal trend or comparative information.
0%	■ No systematic approach to category/item; anecdotal information on approach and implementation; not part of the culture of the student organization.	■ No documented results or poor results. ■ No documented comparisons.

☺ **Idea:** _____

_____

_____

_____

_____

_____

_____

_____

_____

_____

_____

_____

_____

Does your organization have a navigation system?

Where is your organization headed?

How are you going to get there?

Does anyone have a map?

A clear planning process with maximum involvement is necessary for a successful student organization.

✓ **Check it out:** Look in the *AISO Guide for Students* at pages 11–14 for more information on this topic.

☺ **Idea:** _____

_____

_____

_____

_____

_____

_____

_____

_____

_____

_____

_____

_____

Strategic Planning Imperatives

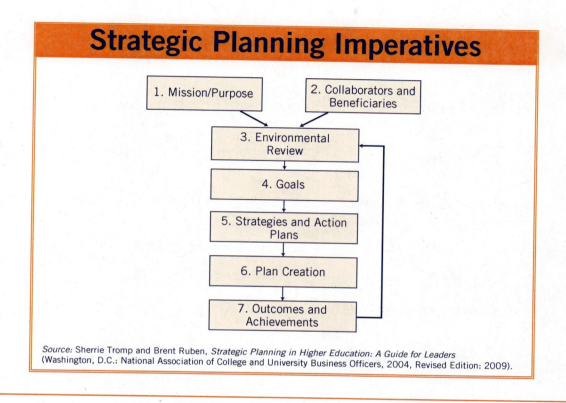

Source: Sherrie Tromp and Brent Ruben, *Strategic Planning in Higher Education: A Guide for Leaders* (Washington, D.C.: National Association of College and University Business Officers, 2004, Revised Edition: 2009).

✔ **Check it out:** Look in the *AISO Guide for Students* at pages 12–14 for more information on this topic.

☺ **Idea:** _____

_____

_____

_____

_____

_____

_____

_____

_____

_____

_____

_____

_____

Who are your constituencies?

Those:

who benefit from your organization's programs, services or activities

who influence or are influenced by your organization, its programs or services

who provide resources or expertise essential to the work of your organization

who can choose to use or not use your programs or services

who pay for your programs or services

upon whom your organization's existence depends

whose assessment of your performance and/or programs or services translates into support, or a lack thereof

✔ **Check it out:** Look in the *AISO Guide for Students* at pages 15–20 for more information on this topic.

☺ **Idea:** _____

_____

_____

_____

_____

_____

_____

_____

_____

_____

_____

_____

_____

_____

Constituent Focus Exercise

☐ What external groups or organizations benefit most from, influence or are influenced by your organization and its programs, activities, and/or services?

☐ How do you learn about the needs, expectations, perceptions and experiences of such groups?

☐ What do such groups need and expect from you?

✓ **Check it out:** Look in the *AISO Guide for Students* at pages 18–20 for more information on this topic.

☺ **Idea:** _____

What's your experience?

Has your organization been asked to:

Provide documentation for how student fees are used?

Complete an annual accountability report for a national chapter?

Submit your group or program for a regional or national award?

Provide examples of organizational success for advisors?

✓ **Check it out:** Look in the *AISO Guide for Students* at pages 18–20 for more information on this topic.

☺ **Idea:** _____

_____

_____

_____

_____

_____

_____

_____

_____

_____

_____

_____

_____

_____

_____

By what standards should the quality of your organization be judged?

If the campus student newspaper carried a story about your organization, what would you want that story to say about...

Leadership		
Strategic Planning		
Constituent Focus		
Assessment & Communication		
Membership & Organizational Climate		
Programs, Activities, & Services		

✓ **Check it out:** Look in the *AISO Guide for Students* at pages 18–20 for more information on this topic.

☺ **Idea:** _____

_____

_____

_____

_____

_____

_____

_____

_____

_____

_____

_____

_____

Our Membership

How do members feel about the organization?

What issues are on the minds of members?

What do members say about being involved
or associated with the group?

✓ **Check it out:** Look in the *AISO Guide for Students* at page 20 for more information on this topic.

☺ **Idea:** _____

_____

_____

_____

_____

_____

_____

_____

_____

_____

_____

_____

_____

What membership groups are being considered in this review?

- ☐ What membership groups might be considered?
  - ■ Active members?
  - ■ All members?
  - ■ Past members?
- ☐ What insights and perspectives can each of these groups provide?
- ☐ Are all of these groups to be included in this review?
- ☐ If some groups will be excluded, why?

✔ **Check it out:** Look in the *AISO Guide for Students* at pages 22–25 for more information on this topic.

☺ **Idea:** _____

_____

_____

_____

_____

_____

_____

_____

_____

_____

_____

_____

_____

Examples of Organizational Climate Issues

Communication
Collaboration
Diversity of membership
Active engagement
Growth and self-development
Recognition

☐ **Does the organization:**
- ■ Facilitate communication and collaboration between individuals within the organization?
- ■ Reflect a culture of respect, equity, teamwork, and collaboration?
- ■ Encourage empowerment and delegation?
- ■ Sustain a sense of community through interaction?

☐ **Is it:**
- ■ Responsive to a diversity of ideas and perspectives?
- ■ Conducive to ongoing improvement?
- ■ Perceived to be a good group with which to be associated?

Source: Rutgers University, Center for Organizational Development and Leadership, *Organizational Climate Inventory* (Washington, D.C.: National Association of College and University Business Officers, 2006).

✔ **Check it out:** Look in the *AISO Guide for Students* at pages 27–30 for more information on this topic.

☺ **Idea:** _____

_____
_____
_____
_____
_____
_____
_____
_____
_____
_____
_____

Process Matrix Exercise

☐ List and briefly describe your mission-critical programs, activities, and services.

☐ List three of the most important processes* associated with each.

☐ For which of the programs/services are the most important processes standardized and documented?

☐ Are the outcomes of these processes regularly evaluated and improved?

☐ Are comparisons with peers and leaders used for process innovation and improvement?

*A process is documented when the steps and responsible individuals or groups are identified. This documentation is easily accessible by the membership. "Mental documentation" does not count!

✔ **Check it out:** Look in the *AISO Guide for Students* at pages 32–34 for more information on this topic.

☺ **Idea:** _____

_____

_____

_____

_____

_____

_____

_____

_____

_____

_____

_____

Mission-Critical Programs, Services, and Activities and Associated Processes Matrix

Mission-Critical Programs, Services, & Activities* (List)	Associated Processes* (List)	Standardized, Documented, Regularly Reviewed? (Y/N)	Outcomes Evaluated? (Y/N)	Comparisons with Other Organizations? (Y/N)

*Processes that are essential to your organization's mission.

✔ **Check it out:** Look in the *AISO Guide for Students* at pages 32–34 for more information on this topic.

☺ **Idea:** _____

_____

_____

_____

_____

_____

_____

_____

_____

_____

_____

_____

_____

_____

Operational and Support Services and Processes Matrix

Mission-Critical Programs, Activities, & Services (List)	Associated Processes* (List)	Standardized, Documented, Regularly Reviewed? (Y/N)	Outcomes Evaluated? (Y/N)	Comparisons with Other Organizations? (Y/N)

*Processes that are important to support your mission-critical programs, activities, and services.

✓ **Check it out:** Look in the *AISO Guide for Students* at pages 32–34 for more information on this topic.

☺ **Idea:** _____

_____

Outcomes and Achievements

☐ What does the evidence indicate? Considering your current outcomes and achievements—and comparisons with your own previous accomplishments, and with those of peers and leaders—how successful is your organization in achieving and sustaining excellence in the following areas?

- Programs, activities, and services
- Constituent groups and organizations
- Membership satisfaction and organizational climate
- Operations and resources

✓ **Check it out:** Look in the *AISO Guide for Students* at pages 35–41 for more information on this topic.

☺ **Idea:** _____

_____
_____
_____
_____
_____
_____
_____
_____
_____
_____
_____

Category 4 and Category 7

An Analogy: Your "Report Card"

Your Report Card

Category 4

- On what should you be graded?

Category 7

- What grade did you get?
- Are you improving over time?
- How do you compare with others?

-Reading [A][ ][ ]

-Writing [B-][ ][ ]

-Math [B][ ][ ]

-Plays well with others [C][ ][ ]

✔ **Check it out:** Look in the *AISO Guide for Students* at pages 35–41 for more information on this topic.

☺ **Idea:** _____

_____

_____

_____

_____

_____

_____

_____

_____

_____

_____

_____

_____

Outcomes and Achievements

Topics to Be Considered

Programs, Activities and Services

- What are your documented and positive outcomes?
- What are some of your most important improvements, and what was their impact?
- Is trend-over-time information available and favorable?
- Have you undertaken comparisons with other organizations?
- In which areas have you made comparisons?
- Are comparisons documented and favorable?

Membership and Climate

- What are your documented and positive outcomes?
- What are some of your most important improvements, and what was their impact?
- Is trend-over-time information available and favorable?
- Have you undertaken comparisons with other organizations?
- In which areas have you made comparisons?
- Are comparisons documented and favorable?

External Constituent Groups and Organizations

- What are your documented and positive outcomes?
- What are some of your most important improvements, and what was their impact?
- Is trend-over-time information available and favorable?
- Have you undertaken comparisons with other organizations?
- In which areas have you made comparisons?
- Are comparisons documented and favorable?

Operations and Resources

- What are your documented and positive outcomes?
- What are some of your most important improvements, and what was their impact?
- Is trend-over-time information available and favorable?
- Have you undertaken comparisons with other organizations?
- In which areas have you made comparisons?
- Are comparisons documented and favorable?

✔ **Check it out:** Look in the *AISO Guide for Students* at pages 35–41 for more information on this topic.

☺ **Idea:** _____

_____

_____

_____

_____

_____

_____

_____

_____

_____

_____

_____

_____

_____

7.1 Leadership – an example

Excellence Indicators (What we *currently* measure)	Outcomes for This Year (+/–/Flat?)	Compared with Prior Years (+/–/Flat?)	Compared with Plans and Goals (+/–/Flat?)	Compared with Peers and Leaders (+/–/Flat?)
■ Using our statement of purpose or vision in marketing	■ Increase strategies (+)	F	F	+
■ Frequency of membership listserv updates	■ Add a summer distribution (+)	+	+	–
■ Officers volunteering as peer advisors for Academic Service department	■ 2 officers volunteer (+)	+	+	+
■ Officers or chairs presenting workshops at NACA regional/national conference	■ One session at each (+)	–	–	+
Wish List (What we would *ideally* measure) *Feedback from general members on elected leaders*				

✔ **Check it out:** Look in the *AISO Guide for Students* at pages 35–41 for more information on this topic.

☺ **Idea:** _____

_____

_____

_____

_____

_____

_____

_____

_____

_____

_____

_____

_____

7.1 Leadership

Excellence Indicators (What we *currently* measure)	Outcomes for This Year (+/–/Flat?)	Compared with Prior Years (+/–/Flat?)	Compared with Plans and Goals (+/–/Flat?)	Compared with Peers and Leaders (+/–/Flat?)
Wish List (What we would *ideally* measure)				

✓ **Check it out:** Look in the *AISO Guide for Students* at pages 35–41 for more information on this topic.

☺ **Idea:** _____

_____

_____

_____

_____

_____

_____

_____

_____

_____

_____

_____

_____

7.2 Strategic Planning

Excellence Indicators (What we *currently* measure)	Outcomes for This Year (+/–/Flat?)	Compared with Prior Years (+/–/Flat?)	Compared with Plans and Goals (+/–/Flat?)	Compared with Peers and Leaders (+/–/Flat?)
Wish List (What we would *ideally* measure)				

✔ **Check it out:** Look in the *AISO Guide for Students* at pages 35–41 for more information on this topic.

☺ **Idea:** _____

_____

_____

_____

_____

_____

_____

_____

_____

_____

_____

_____

_____

7.3 Constituencies

Excellence Indicators (What we *currently* measure)	Outcomes for This Year (+/–/Flat?)	Compared with Prior Years (+/–/Flat?)	Compared with Plans and Goals (+/–/Flat?)	Compared with Peers and Leaders (+/–/Flat?)
Wish List (What we would *ideally* measure)				

✔ **Check it out:** Look in the *AISO Guide for Students* at pages 35–41 for more information on this topic.

☺ **Idea:** _____

_____

_____

_____

_____

_____

_____

_____

_____

_____

_____

_____

7.4.A Programs, Activities and Services (Mission-Critical)

Excellence Indicators (What we *currently* measure)	Outcomes for This Year (+/–/Flat?)	Compared with Prior Years (+/–/Flat?)	Compared with Plans and Goals (+/–/Flat?)	Compared with Peers and Leaders (+/–/Flat?)
Wish List (What we would *ideally* measure)				

✔ **Check it out:** Look in the *AISO Guide for Students* at pages 35–41 for more information on this topic.

☺ **Idea:** _____

_____
_____
_____
_____
_____
_____
_____
_____
_____
_____
_____

7.4.B Services (Operations and Resources)

Excellence Indicators (What we *currently* measure)	Outcomes for This Year (+/–/Flat?)	Compared with Prior Years (+/–/Flat?)	Compared with Plans and Goals (+/–/Flat?)	Compared with Peers and Leaders (+/–/Flat?)
Wish List (What we would *ideally* measure)				

✔ **Check it out:** Look in the *AISO Guide for Students* at pages 35–41 for more information on this topic.

☺ **Idea:** _____

7.5 Membership and Organizational Climate

Excellence Indicators (What we *currently* measure)	Outcomes for This Year (+/–/Flat?)	Compared with Prior Years (+/–/Flat?)	Compared with Plans and Goals (+/–/Flat?)	Compared with Peers and Leaders (+/–/Flat?)
Wish List (What we would *ideally* measure)				

✓ **Check it out:** Look in the *AISO Guide for Students* at pages 35–41 for more information on this topic.

☺ **Idea:** _____

_____

_____

_____

_____

_____

_____

_____

_____

_____

_____

_____

_____

7.6 Assessment and Communication

Excellence Indicators (What we *currently* measure)	Outcomes for This Year (+/–/Flat?)	Compared with Prior Years (+/–/Flat?)	Compared with Plans and Goals (+/–/Flat?)	Compared with Peers and Leaders (+/–/Flat?)
Wish List (What we would *ideally* measure)				

✔ **Check it out:** Look in the *AISO Guide for Students* at pages 35–41 for more information on this topic.

☺ **Idea:** _____

_____

_____

_____

_____

_____

_____

_____

_____

_____

_____

_____

_____

Creating Project Improvement Plans and Teams

For each improvement area selected as a priority by the group, develop an action plan by specifying the following:

Sponsor(s): _____ Project leader: _____

Project description: _____

_____

Action steps: Project members:
1.   •
2.   •
3.   •
                                 •

Funding considerations: _____

Communication considerations: _____

Deliverables: _____

Time frame: _____

Project effectiveness measure(s): _____

☺ Idea: _____

_____

_____

_____

_____

_____

_____

_____

_____

_____

_____

_____

_____

_____

_____

_____

_____

Resources

☐ If your student group has questions regarding the AISO assessment process, contact:

☐ **Dr. Brent D. Ruben**
- ■ Center for Organizational Development & Leadership
- ■ 732/932-3020 ext. 4024
- ■ ruben@odl.rutgers.edu

☐ **Tricia Nolfi**
- ■ University Human Resources
- ■ 732/942-3020 ext. 4075
- ■ tnolfi@hr.rutgers.edu